BECOMING OLD

 A catalogue record for this book is available from the National Library of Australia

© Richard Greene

Published 2021

ISBN: 978-0-6453006-6-6 (epub)
ISBN: 978-0-6453006-7-3 (paperback)
ISBN: 978-0-6453006-8-0 (PDF)

Published with the aid of Jumble Books and Publishers (jumblebooksandpublishers.com)

Image credit:
Goya - Old Man on a Swing, Bordeaux Album II, (1824-28). Hispanic Society of America, New York by Francisco de Goya (1746-1828), 1824.
Image is in the public domain.

Becoming Old

Poems of Aging

by

Richard Greene

Richard Greene is a poet, or has been at least since he retired from a 38-year career in international development. A lawyer by training, he fell into his development career by accident when, after law school, though planning not to practice law but interested in international affairs, he accepted an unsolicited job offer from the U.S. Agency for International Development. After a few years in Washington (or Foggy Bottom, as the location of the U.S. foreign policy establishment is known), he was assigned as legal advisor to the USAID mission in Laos and there discovered that the development business suited his interests and inclinations very well.

Greene wrote poetry beginning in the 8th grade and continued through college where he studied with a Professor, Henry Rago, who later became editor of *Poetry* magazine, the leading U.S. poetry journal. However, he wrote few poems after law school as he became absorbed in international development, but turned back to poetry as he neared retirement.

To all those who, like myself, are in or approaching their twilight years.

Contents

I See Myself Becoming Old 1
On the Downhill Side 2
My Third Grade Playmates 3
Reunion 4
The Cookie 5
You Can Tell Us by Our Pecs 6
Planned Obsolescence 7
How I Know I'm Getting Old 8
Medicine Man 9
Waiting 10
These Hands 11
The Incredible Shrinking Man 12
In Denial 13
Them and Us 14
A Voice from the Past 15
Insouciance 16
Old Men Don't Care What They Wear 17
Pas de Deux 18
Reveille 19
The Girls of Summer 20
The Way We Were 21
Still the Same 22
Packing Up 23
Afternoon at the Movies 25
A Special Theory of Relativity 26
End of an Era 27
The World Is Dwindling 28

Their Jungle Gym Is Overgrown with Vines 29
A Cry in the Night 30
Judgment Day 31
Assisted Living 32
What's a Century? 33
79th Birthday 34
Aliens 35
Forever Young 36
The Circle Closes 37
Running Down 38
It's Hard to Believe We Were Ever So Young 39
Long Day's Journey into Suppertime 40
Cantankerous 41
Ossuary 42

I See Myself Becoming Old

My closet is full of suits I don't wear anymore.
Nothing I need to wear them for.
There are days when I stay in my pajamas till noon.
I picture my heirs looking at my wardrobe one day
asking "Can you think of anyone who can use these
or should we give them to Goodwill?"
Or, "Would you like this tie as a remembrance of
   Dad?"
As I read the obits of the recently deceased,
which I took to doing a few years ago,
I compare their ages to mine.

Then there's the arthritis in my hands and feet.
My left foot aches when I walk
and I suffered a rupture in a time-worn tendon not
   long ago.
I have more trouble lifting things and getting
   around.
Don't jump over puddles anymore
for fear of the damage I might do coming down.
(No more kicking up heels for me.)

What will it be next,
the incipient cataracts?
My hearing isn't what it used to be.
I don't think I need a hearing aid yet,
though my daughter disagrees.
Or will it be something unforeseen
like that ill-fated tendon?

I see myself becoming old,
yet it's as if I were watching it happen to somebody
   else.

On the Downhill Side

April is almost over
having, it seems, only just begun.
Once past the apex
we speed ever faster.
Ascending was slower
The landscape labored by.
Each time you rounded a curve
there was another just ahead
and you never saw the summit
much less the decline on the other side.
Then one day you notice you're on the downgrade.
The landscape unreels
at an accelerating pace.
You glimpse lowlands in the distance
from time to time
but the road
absorbed in its curves
never reveals its destination.
Down you go
wind pressed to your face,
applying the brakes
which no longer work the way they used to
and the last thing on your mind
is to shout whoopee.

My Third Grade Playmates

My third grade playmates are 68.
Smooth skin has withered.
Nimble bodies have grown tentative.
Voices once fluting now grate.
Dreams have curdled.
Ambition is in disrepair.
They are full of memories
and in memory they are preserved.
The children of my memory
are old.

Reunion

I went to my wife's 50th high school reunion last
    night.
Lithe bodies grown lumpy,
once smooth countenances sagging,
successes and failures worn on faces.
I imagined the young people in the yearbook
changing before my eyes,
as if in time-lapse cinematography,
through intervening stages
to the gray-haired empty nesters in the room,
but I saw in their eyes
a rebirth of those vanished youths.

The Cookie

Once I was dough
waiting to be shaped.
Then I was baked
and after
I was moist and chewy,
but over time I dried out,
and now I'm beginning to crumble.

You Can Tell Us by Our Pecs

I'm a septuagenarian
almost an octo
and many a celebrity's
in my age group now.
We're what they call a cohort,
nearing the end of our long march.
Catching a glimpse of myself in the bathroom
    mirror
as I dried after showering this morning
I was reminded of pictures I saw on the cover
of one of those journals you find
on supermarket checkout lines,
Clint Eastwood, Alec Baldwin
and Arnold Schwarzenegger
in swimsuits,
all with breasts like pubescent girls.

Planned Obsolescence

My hands no longer work the way they used to.
They ache this morning
and I had trouble opening a jar.
Problems too with my wrists, eyes, feet,
shins, shoulders, sacroiliac.
I've had my body in the shop
several times of late
but the wheels still squeak
the steering's loose
and it chugs when going uphill.
Trade-in, however, isn't an option.

How I Know I'm Getting Old

When I was young
and the Andrews Sisters were popular
I couldn't imagine what people saw in them.
I didn't care for their songs
or three-part harmony.
But basically it was what they stood for in my mind.
Though I knew no Andrews Sisters fans
I could imagine what they were like:
people who lived in tacky subdivisions
and voted for Eisenhower,
women with perms
who waxed orgasmic
over refrigerators,
and said things like
"Ladies first" and
"That's what little girls are made of."

Now when I hear the Andrews sisters sing
"Bei Mir Bist Du Schein",
or "The Boogie Woogie Bugle Boy of Company B",
nostalgia creeps over me.

Medicine Man

I've arrived at the age of medicines.
Every morning I arrange a bouquet
of varying sizes, shapes, colors, textures,
    transparencies.
You are what you eat, they say.
I picture a man made of pills and capsules
like a sculpture composed of found objects
by some Picasso of the medicine chest.

I remember seeing my grandparents,
and then my parents,
setting out their daily array of medications.
I didn't give it much thought at the time
but now I know it defines the old,
and I've become one of them.

Most of my life it's been "them".
One doesn't think of oneself
as destined to be old
For that matter, one doesn't quite believe it
when it happens.
I see the signs
but their significance escapes me.
My body may be old,
but not me.

Waiting

I am waiting for the rest of my hair to turn gray
and I am waiting for the next medicine I will be
    taking
for the rest of my life.
I am waiting for my hearing to get so bad
I'll really need a hearing aid
though some think I need one now,
and I am waiting for my cataracts to flower.
I am waiting for another CAT scan or MRI
and especially another colonoscopy.
I am waiting for my face and butt to sag
my procreative organ to lose completely
its power to stand up
and my libido to retire
(but not holding my breath).
I am waiting for my memory to head south,
like snowbirds.
I am just waiting to use a walker,
and I am waiting for the grim reaper
to tap me on the shoulder,
but not yet.

These Hands

These hands have been shuffling cards
for more than seventy years.
The motion's still the same
but the skin is slacker,
hangs looser on the bones,
is spotted.

These hands have punched and pounded,
caressed and petted,
rubbed, tickled, scratched,
wiped bottoms, fastened diapers,
fed hungry mouths,
sliced, diced, peeled and poured,
made shadow animals
and here's the church and here's the steeple,
played instruments,
written and typed,
opened books, turned pages,
gripped, grabbed, cupped, pointed,
folded, gestured,
saluted, made obscene gestures,
pulled triggers, stanched wounds,
tied and untied,
buttoned, zipped
unbuttoned, unzipped,
unhooked…

These feet too have begun to shuffle, but only
    recently,
The hands, however, busily carry on, much as
    always,
though there are some things they no longer do.

The Incredible Shrinking Man

I

My skin is becoming all wrinkles
like an elephant's.
When I hold my arm at a certain angle
it looks like ripples in sand
for I'm shrinking inside my skin.
Becoming a wrinkly homunculus is what I am.

II

I've lost three inches since my prime.
I'm still five foot ten
but well on my way to becoming a little old man,
something I never envisioned in my youth.
If you asked young people "Do you think you'll live
    forever?"
they'd answer "Of course not. What a silly
    question."
but the fact is they can't conceive of growing old.

In Denial

Since reaching its mid-seventies
my body's started to decay
at an accelerated pace.
It's not like the illnesses of youth
from which one recovers
but permanent conditions that accumulate,
a muscle that's lost its tendon
an eye that drifts
a foot that flaps
a persistent pain in the backside
an organ removed by surgeons
taking some functions with it.
But though my body may act its age
in my mind I still feel young,
about eighteen sometimes,
rarely over forty-five.
I suppose you could say I'm in denial.
Isn't that the best response?

Them and Us

The young can't know
what it's like getting old.
What it's like to grow up, yes.
Being grown-up has its attractions.
But being old
with its slowness and infirmities?
It merely excites impatience.
So for most of our lives the old are them.
Then one day they're us
and we can't understand
the inability of the young
to empathize.

A Voice from the Past

Talking to an old friend on the phone
I hear the voice of the youth he was
sixty some years ago.
Though he sounds his age,
the voice on the phone
is overlaid with the one I knew,
as if his words were propelled
across not just space but time as well.

Insouciance

I saw an old man by the road
tinkering with his mailbox.
He wore just a robe
leather shoes and dark sox
and his calves were bare
but he showed no sign
of self-consciousness.
Such is the freedom of being old.

Old Men Don't Care What They Wear

They dress for ease and comfort
or with whatever comes readily to hand.
Today I wore tennis shoes
to a restaurant named Demarchelier.
The headwaiter looked down his nose
at which point he might have spied dark sox
if I hadn't happened to have opened the drawer
with white ones.
I'd wear ties that are too wide or narrow
if I bothered to wear ties,
my suits were fashionable a generation back
and the style of my eyeglasses
is almost as out of date.
I often stay in my pajamas all day.
I may wear a T-shirt to the pearly gates
and hope St. Peter isn't persnickety
but if he is
I know a less uptight place.

Pas de Deux

I have a neighbor
who's in his eighties I'd say.
He's frosted all over
slightly stooped
and walks with a cane.
He has a little white dog
that matches him in dog years
with that stiff gait old dogs have.
I see them walking together
several times a day,
tottering down the path,
to oblivion.

Reveille

I'm going through one of those bouts of insomnia
to which the old are prone.
I turn my arthritic body over in bed
at four or five AM
and can't get back to sleep
so I get up and read the morning *Times* online.
I also see the dawn
that most of my life I've rarely seen.
This morning it's cloudless
and at this hour
a burnt orange fringe
swells symphonically over the eastern hills.
It takes me back to my days in basic training
one of the few times when I was often up at dawn
and I feel in my 80-year-old flesh the sensation
of being the young soldier I was then.

The Girls of Summer

The lodge where we stayed last night
had iron in its water
like our house at the lake
where I spent my childhood summers
and as I was falling asleep,
one thing leading to another,
I thought of the Hutchinson girls
with their blond hair and bouncy curls.
seeing them in my mind's eye
on the lawn
between their big house and the breakwater.
The youngest was in her early teens
and I a couple of years younger.
They were my American dream.

They're probably grandmothers now,
if still among the living.

The Way We Were

We were at a party the other night
and our gray-haired hostess was telling us
how she'd moved to town.
"I was pregnant at the time," she said,
and it occurred to me
that one seldom thinks of the elderly
as ever having had sex.
It's as if their children were immaculately
    conceived.
But what we are today
isn't what we were once upon a time
and she who now seems a paragon of propriety
might in her youth have been
disconcertingly passionate.

Still the Same

Somewhere are young women
I once knew
some 50 years ago,
still young
still the same,
unwrinkled
slender
supple,
hair still glossy
voices velvety…
somewhere in the lanes and alleys of my brain.

Packing Up

Today I helped a friend who's moving
from a place he's lived in for twenty years.
He asked me to sort through old papers
saving those that told a story
throwing away the rest.
This is what he was doing
when I arrived
while his grown children were packing the kitchen,
but he was doing it slowly,
too slowly for his offspring,
reading each document pensively.

It's not just that he's moving.
He's old.
It struck me
as I watched him bent over his papers
holding them close to his face
reading without his glasses
his eyes looking older
with no lenses to hide their age.
When he got up after a while
he put his hand to his back
and stooped as he walked away.

So he sifted through his life's detritus
as I looked over his shoulder
like an angel on judgment day,
his life laid out in those papers,
memos and letters from work,
a letter from a child's principal,
deeds,
a divorce decree.
At first as I read on my own

the documents were exotic to me,
as if they concerned someone I didn't know.
Then I came to the place where our lives
   converged.
Now we're together once more,
in the fraternity of age.

Afternoon at the Movies

Life, which for the young unfolds so slowly,
for the old unravels all too fast.
Children and youths,
we waited out each year impatiently,
ever eager to reach the next,
to add another number to our age,
to go from elementary to junior high,
to high school,
to college,
to be of driving age,
to be tall,
to reach menarche,
or lose our virginity.

Looking forward, we seemed to approach those
    milestones
in slow motion.
Looking back, they race by in a blur.
Life, which once seemed an endless scroll,
I hold now in my hand
a slender book.
Visiting my daughter in a place where the young
    abound
I see them all about me in a mating dance
while I remember my wooing days
as if no more than a picture show
viewed in a few hours one afternoon.

A Special Theory of Relativity

As I grow old
everything seems to move faster.
It still takes the Earth
three hundred and sixty-five days
to circle the sun,
but a year doesn't seem as long as it used to.
Tomorrow is Friday
but it feels like Monday was yesterday.
It's as if summer has been over for just a few weeks
and already it's nearly Thanksgiving.
My next birthday's just around the corner
but it seems like the last was just a few months ago.
The days go by like pages being riffled.
Soon I'll come to the end of the book.

End of an Era

Anita O'Day died yesterday
When I heard it on public radio
I told my daughter
and she said
"Who's Anita O'Day?"
Is this what it means for an era to end?

The World Is Dwindling

It used to be that when some celebrity
of my parents' generation died
I thought, without much feeling,
it's just old times receding.
Now that I'm the older generation
each time a well-known person of my cohort passes
    away
it feels like a piece of the world has broken off.

Their Jungle Gym Is Overgrown with Vines

In the house
there's a bedroom, I imagine,
or more than one perhaps,
preserved as a museum
on the walls, posters of decades past,
surfaces otherwise uncluttered,
beds always neatly made,
and those who remain behind,
their hair gradually turning gray.

A Cry in the Night

I was awakened by the sound
of a child crying Daddy
but when I awoke I realized
it was only a dream,
for no child has called for me in the night
in almost forty years.

Judgment Day

My mother-in-law,
moving soon to a nursing home,
sits at our dining room table
sorting papers
tearing some into small pieces
and throwing them into a large black bag,
placing a select few
in a small box.

Assisted Living

She lives in a "studio" now
at what used to be called
an old people's home
surrounded there by a winnowing
of the household where her children came of age,
a dresser, a sofa, some armchairs
pictures
bric-a-brac,
like those Chinese figurines
that accompanied important personages to the
    grave,
a lifetime in fabric, wood and porcelain
each object with its story,
a vacation perhaps
maybe a trip abroad
maybe just a shopping trip,
things acquired with pleasure and pride
as if a life could be portrayed
like sculpture fashioned of found objects.

And in a hall nearby
a crowd of residents
listen to a buxom woman sing
songs of earlier generations,
all facing the singer
as if seated on a train
watching the scenery go by
waiting for that final destination.

What's a Century?

The receptionist asks me my date of birth.
"March 23, 1931", I say
and think how remote that must seem
to the young woman behind the desk
in this year of our lord 2006.
Somebody born a century earlier than me
would have arrived in the Jackson presidency,
the first not of a founding father or one's son,
before the coming of the radio, the car, the
    airplane, the great building of railroads,
the war that almost split our young nation in two.
At my age, that man born 100 years before me
would have found himself in a wondrously different
    world
from that into which he came,
the modern world for all its later change.
But here I stand before this young woman
a representative of an era three quarters of a
    century past
and she probably gives it no thought.
In her job, she meets septuagenarians every day.
Besides, the young are seldom interested
in their parents' or grandparents' times
until it's too late.

79th Birthday

Another year
and I'll be 80,
eight decades on this planet,
mere seconds for humankind,
nanoseconds for Gaia,
but for the young
my childhood years
are history.

Aliens

So I complete my eightieth year.
I've joined the nation of the agèd.
For most of my years
I couldn't imagine being old.
Those who were seemed to me
like creatures from another planet,
old throughout their lives.
But now it's the young who are alien
and I look on them with wonder
at the time warp in which they exist.

Forever Young

Though I've passed the scriptural three score and
    ten
I don't feel old inside my skin.
My legs don't falter.
My hands don't shake.
My eyes don't water.
My mind doesn't stray.
I feel in the driver's seat
up here in my brain.
In fact I feel about nineteen,
still given to enthusiasms,
still remembering mistakes.

The Circle Closes

    I

We bought a child gate the other day
at Toys-R-Us,
the kind you use to keep a toddler
from getting into dangerous places
or falling down the stairs.
The week before it was an infant monitor
used to hear your child cry from another room
or maybe breathe, if you're the anxious sort.
They were for my mother-in-law.
She's living with us now
and we cut her food for her on her plate.

    II

Time was when I had no memories,
or words,
then just a few,
was cradle-bound
then crawled, then toddled
before walking like a man.
Time was when I counted birthdays eagerly.

Now my memory has sprung a leak
and words, I find, sometimes elude my grasp,
few breaths remain to me
for blowing out the candles on a cake,
I limp some days
and can see
a walker in my future,
before I toddle, totter, shuffle
out of sight.

Running Down

Eyes too dim
to read a book
or even watch TV,
he now runs memories
in the cinema of his mind.

It's Hard to Believe We Were Ever So Young

Looking through old photos.
Cousin Sue and I in Chicago
in front of one of those courtyard buildings
recognizably of the place and time.
I must have been four,
Sue eleven.
She's now eighty-six.

Myself, sixteen, with my Uncle Sam
and cousin Siggie
on that fishing trip
to the remote Canadian lakes
where the rivers drain into Hudson's Bay,
Uncle Sam and Siggie
now both deceased.

My sister with her firstborn
on the hill behind our family farm
wearing her father's World War I campaign hat
with a pheasant feather stuck in the band
her son toddling beside her.
He's now forty-six.

Myself with long brown hair,
sideburns, moustache and granny glasses
cradling my infant daughter in one arm.
She's now thirty-nine.

Long Day's Journey into Suppertime

Not much drama to my days.
Retired.
No longer jousting in the way of the young
needing to prove themselves.
Beyond the hurdles of the mating game,
tranquil in a marriage not in the least tempestuous.
Children grown.
Not worry free (if such exist in the parental mind)
but doing OK.

Little social life.
Never really cared for it.
Seldom go to the movies or even watch TV.
Bored?
Not a bit.
Attend to family business, meticulously,
in a way not possible in my busy years,
exercise diligently,
do the grocery shopping,
cook for myself and my wife who works,
read, study even,
email of course,
spend most of my time in my armchair
or at my desk,
venturing forth when I feel the urge
seldom because I feel I must.
But then,
isn't all drama really in the mind?

Cantankerous

I'd rather be an "old man"
than a "senior citizen."
Old men may be crotchety,
have spots on their clothes.
be ill shaven
but they're all their own,
speak their minds.
Senior citizens join associations.

Senior citizens complain.
Old men cuss.
Old men roam.
Senior citizens go on tours.

Senior citizens may be PC
but I'd rather be cantankerous.

Ossuary

Rubbing my arthritic hands, I notice
the skeleton inside.
It's as though the flesh were retracting
revealing bone,
but more likely
I've merely become conscious,
as befits my age,
of being a soft receptacle
that will soon biodegrade.

www.ingramcontent.com/pod-product-compliance
Lightning Source LLC
Chambersburg PA
CBHW061345040426
42444CB00011B/3093